# My First Book About Backyard Nature

## Donald M. Silver
## & Patricia J. Wynne

Ecology for Kids!

DOVER PUBLICATIONS, INC.
Mineola, New York

Our backyards are filled with thousands of living organisms, and most of us don't even realize it! In this fun and informative coloring book, kids will learn all about the plants and animals that depend upon the backyard to survive. From flowers and trees to insects and birds and mammals, this book tells their stories and how we are all connected in the ecosystem that is Earth.

*For Zach, Gabby, and Cassie Monteau,*
*Who take such good care of the butterflies and birds, frogs and iguana,*
*seashells and dinosaurs in our secret garden.*

*DMS*

*Bibliographical Note*
*My First Book About Backyard Nature: Ecology for Kids!* is a new work,
first published by Dover Publications, Inc., in 2016.

*International Standard Book Number*
*ISBN-13: 978-0-486-80949-6*
*ISBN-10: 0-486-80949-8*

Manufactured in the United States by LSC Communications
80949806    2018
www.doverpublications.com

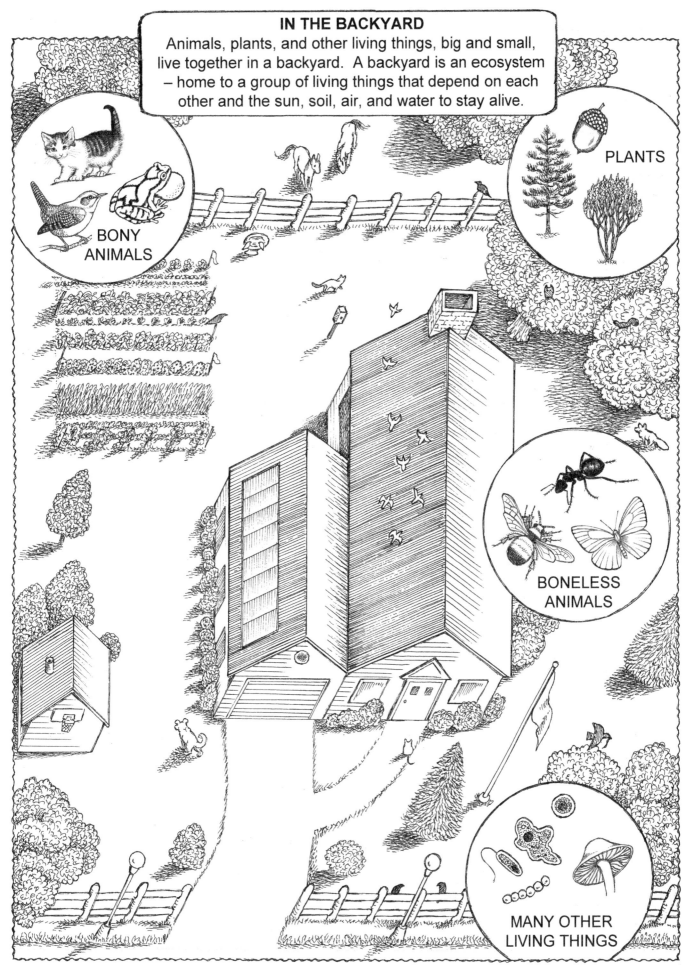

**IN THE BACKYARD**

Animals, plants, and other living things, big and small, live together in a backyard. A backyard is an ecosystem – home to a group of living things that depend on each other and the sun, soil, air, and water to stay alive.

BONY ANIMALS

PLANTS

BONELESS ANIMALS

MANY OTHER LIVING THINGS

1

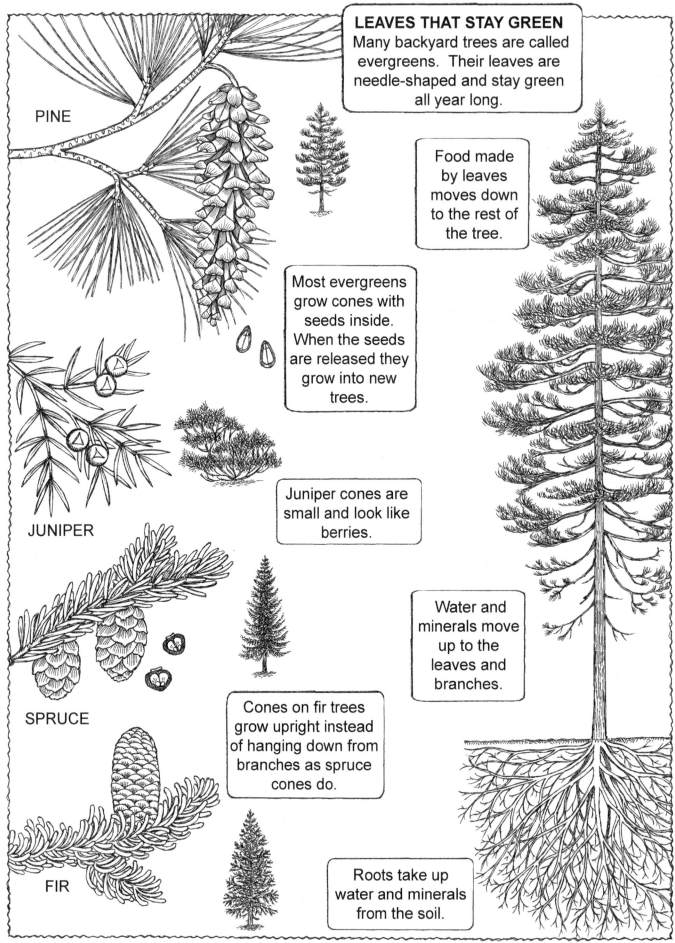

PINE

**LEAVES THAT STAY GREEN**
Many backyard trees are called evergreens. Their leaves are needle-shaped and stay green all year long.

Food made by leaves moves down to the rest of the tree.

Most evergreens grow cones with seeds inside. When the seeds are released they grow into new trees.

JUNIPER

Juniper cones are small and look like berries.

Water and minerals move up to the leaves and branches.

SPRUCE

Cones on fir trees grow upright instead of hanging down from branches as spruce cones do.

FIR

Roots take up water and minerals from the soil.

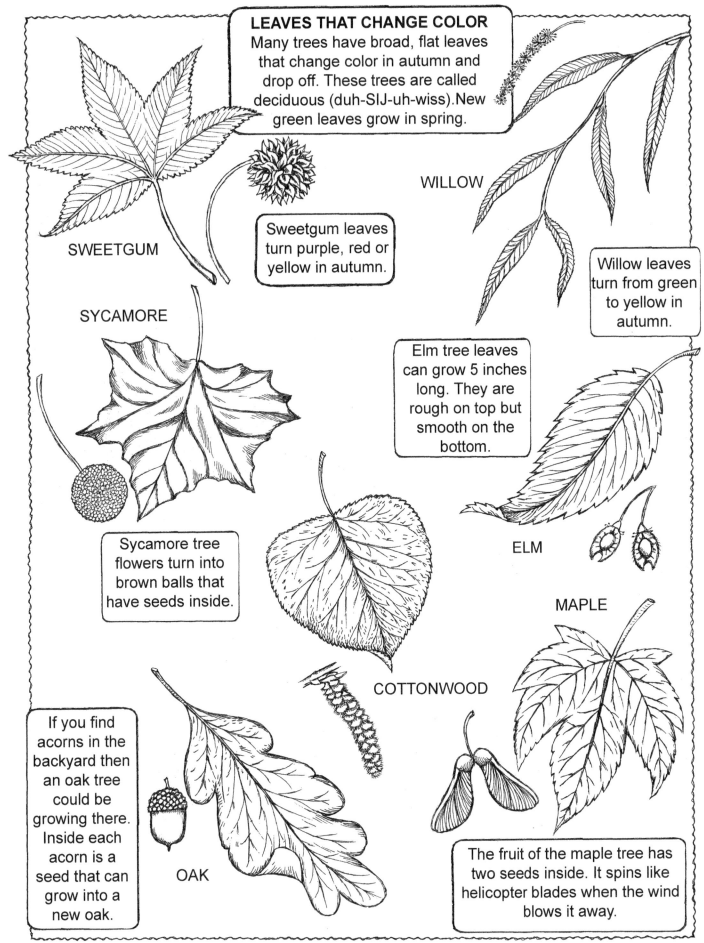

**LEAVES THAT CHANGE COLOR**
Many trees have broad, flat leaves that change color in autumn and drop off. These trees are called deciduous (duh-SIJ-uh-wiss). New green leaves grow in spring.

WILLOW

SWEETGUM

Sweetgum leaves turn purple, red or yellow in autumn.

Willow leaves turn from green to yellow in autumn.

SYCAMORE

Elm tree leaves can grow 5 inches long. They are rough on top but smooth on the bottom.

Sycamore tree flowers turn into brown balls that have seeds inside.

ELM

MAPLE

COTTONWOOD

If you find acorns in the backyard then an oak tree could be growing there. Inside each acorn is a seed that can grow into a new oak.

OAK

The fruit of the maple tree has two seeds inside. It spins like helicopter blades when the wind blows it away.

**GRASS**
Grass grows in most backyards. It is green because it contains chlorophyll for making food, using energy from the sun.

← LEAF

Grass leaves are narrow and are called blades.

Grasshoppers and caterpillars feed on grass.

PRAYING MANTIS

STEM

Grass plants that are eaten or cut keep growing back.

NEW GRASS PLANT

These grass plants send out stems that creep along the ground. New grass plants grow out of these stems.

CREEPING STEM

Grass roots take in water and nutrients that the plant needs to grow.

ROOTS

Brightly colored rhododendron flowers bloom in spring. Though a rhododendron is a bush, it can grow more than 30 feet tall!

Some dogwoods are trees; others are bushes. You can tell this is a tree by its trunk and big flowers.

A blueberry bush will attract mockingbirds, blue jays, and other berry eaters.

Sumacs are bushes and small trees. They grow clusters of fruits that many birds like to eat.

The fuzzy covering on the pussy willow bush flowers protects them from the cold.

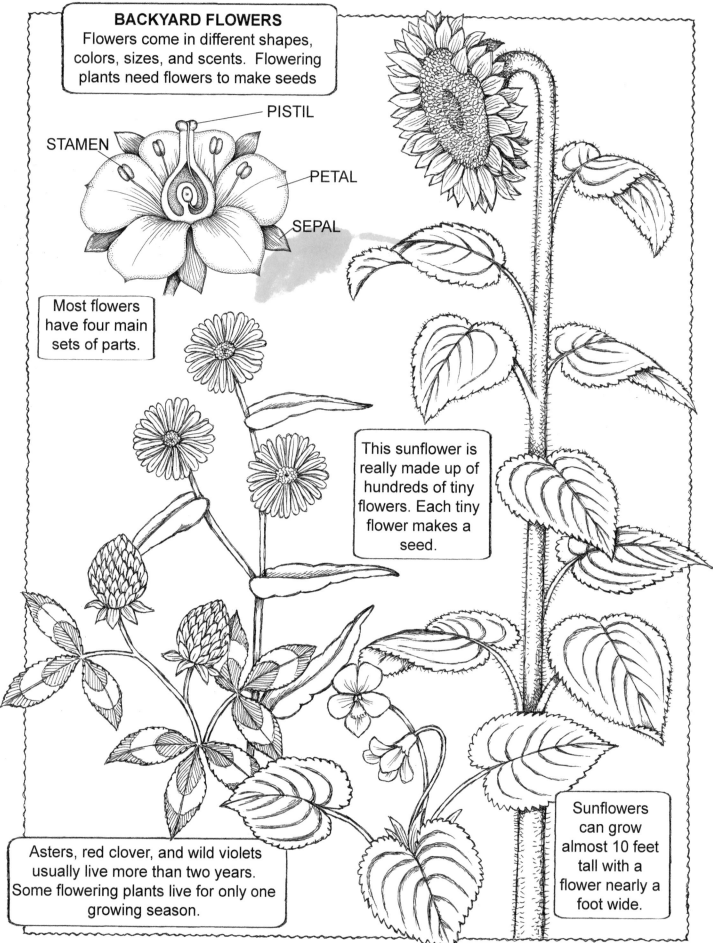

**BACKYARD FLOWERS**
Flowers come in different shapes, colors, sizes, and scents. Flowering plants need flowers to make seeds

PISTIL

STAMEN

PETAL

SEPAL

Most flowers have four main sets of parts.

This sunflower is really made up of hundreds of tiny flowers. Each tiny flower makes a seed.

Sunflowers can grow almost 10 feet tall with a flower nearly a foot wide.

Asters, red clover, and wild violets usually live more than two years. Some flowering plants live for only one growing season.

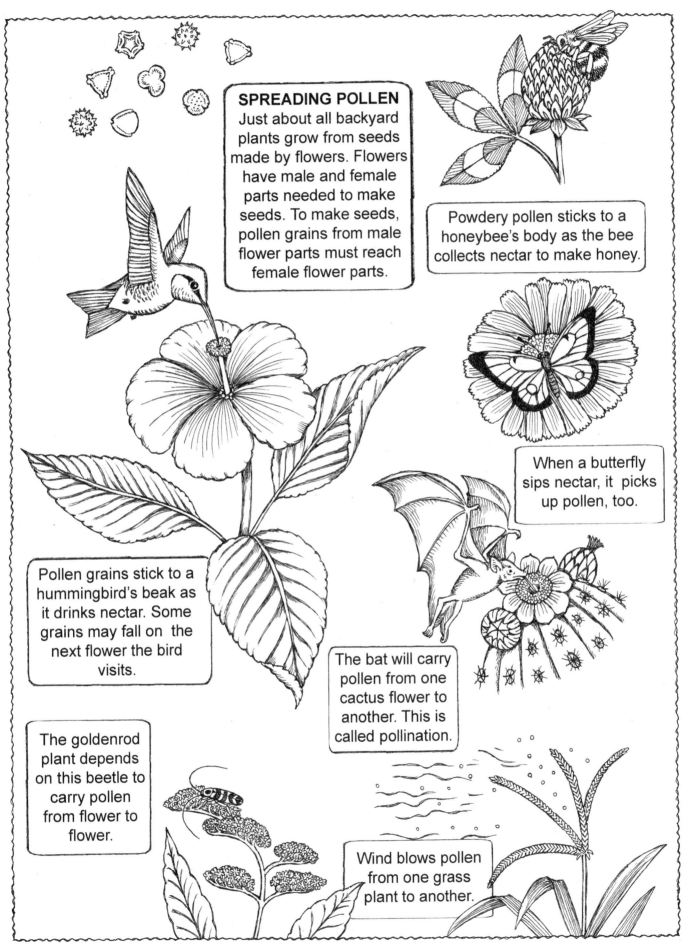

## SPREADING POLLEN

Just about all backyard plants grow from seeds made by flowers. Flowers have male and female parts needed to make seeds. To make seeds, pollen grains from male flower parts must reach female flower parts.

Powdery pollen sticks to a honeybee's body as the bee collects nectar to make honey.

When a butterfly sips nectar, it picks up pollen, too.

Pollen grains stick to a hummingbird's beak as it drinks nectar. Some grains may fall on the next flower the bird visits.

The bat will carry pollen from one cactus flower to another. This is called pollination.

The goldenrod plant depends on this beetle to carry pollen from flower to flower.

Wind blows pollen from one grass plant to another.

7

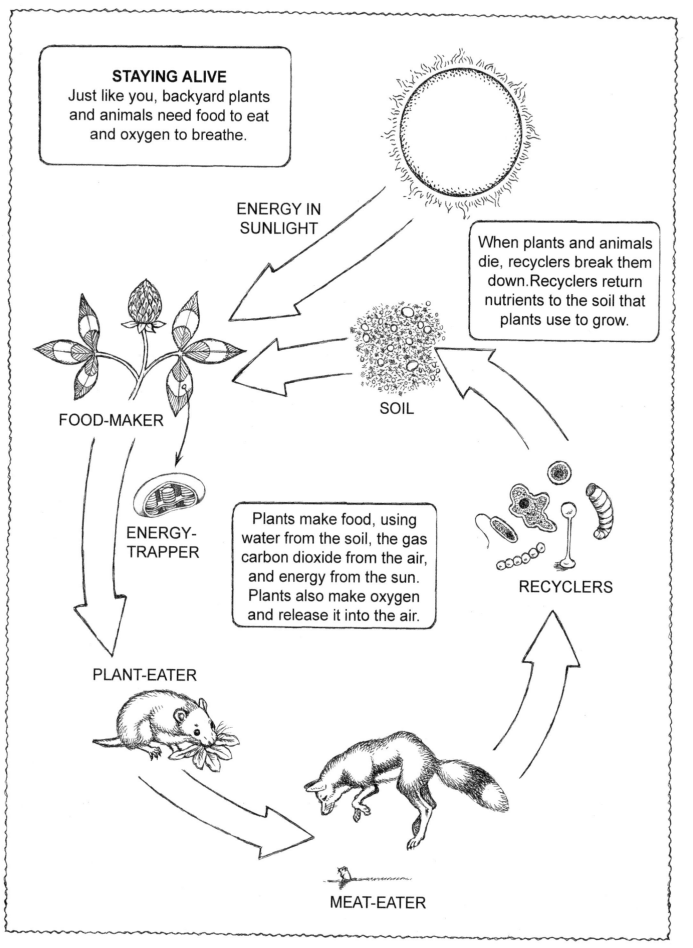

**STAYING ALIVE**
Just like you, backyard plants and animals need food to eat and oxygen to breathe.

ENERGY IN SUNLIGHT

FOOD-MAKER

ENERGY-TRAPPER

PLANT-EATER

MEAT-EATER

SOIL

When plants and animals die, recyclers break them down. Recyclers return nutrients to the soil that plants use to grow.

Plants make food, using water from the soil, the gas carbon dioxide from the air, and energy from the sun. Plants also make oxygen and release it into the air.

RECYCLERS

8

**SPRING**
As the days grow longer and warmer, it often rains. Backyard flowers bloom and leaves start to grow.

The yellow warbler builds a nest on a backyard branch and lays eggs.

Spring rain brings water plants need to grow.

The hummingbird pokes its beak inside a flower in search of sweet nectar.

A skink curls its tail around its eggs.

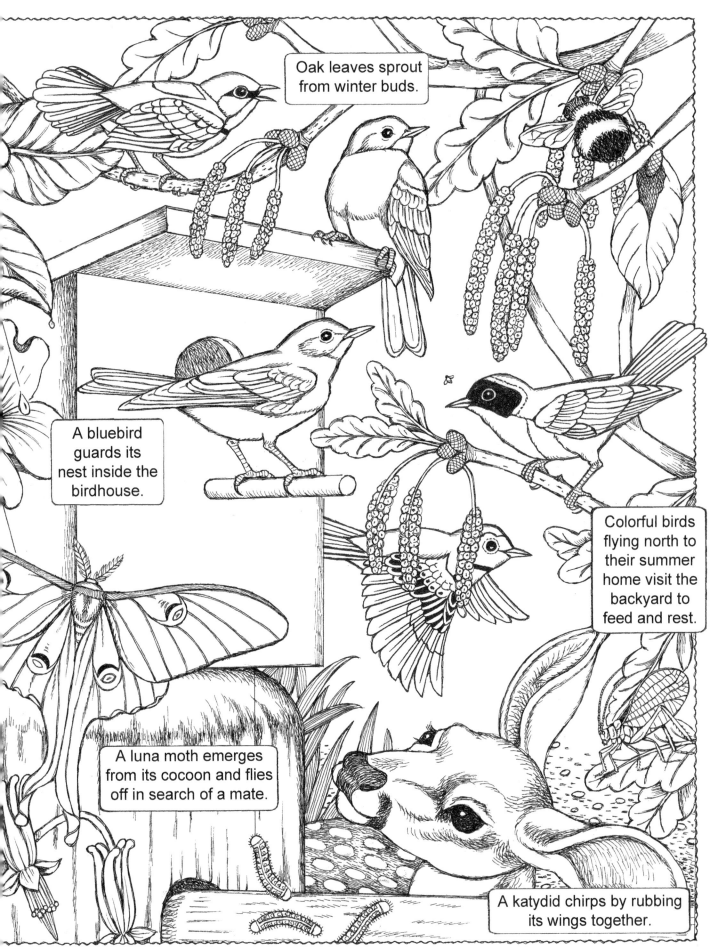

Oak leaves sprout from winter buds.

A bluebird guards its nest inside the birdhouse.

Colorful birds flying north to their summer home visit the backyard to feed and rest.

A luna moth emerges from its cocoon and flies off in search of a mate.

A katydid chirps by rubbing its wings together.

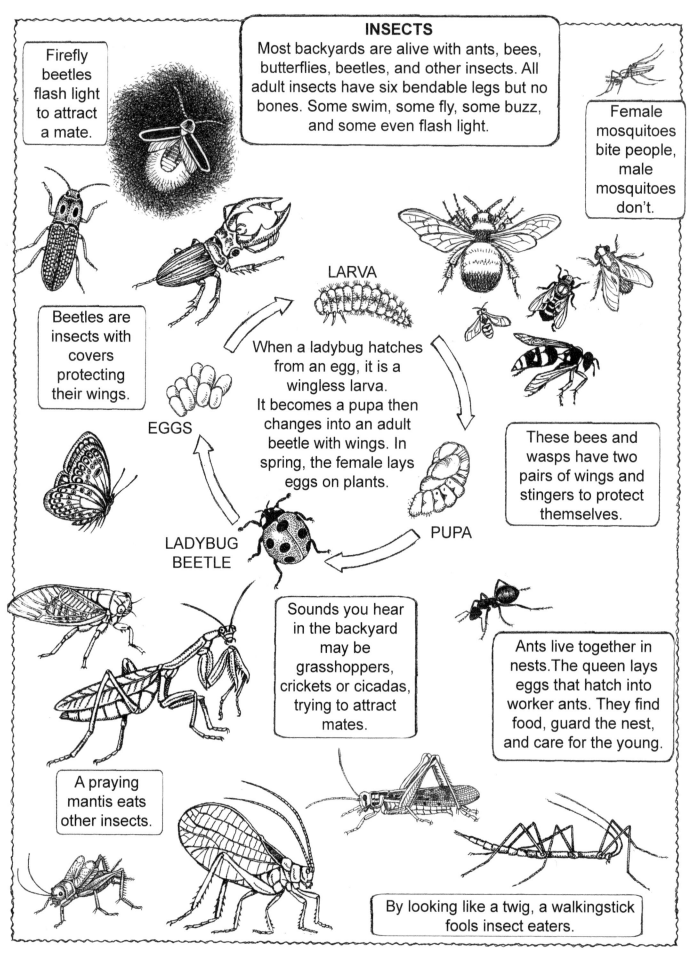

**INSECTS**
Most backyards are alive with ants, bees, butterflies, beetles, and other insects. All adult insects have six bendable legs but no bones. Some swim, some fly, some buzz, and some even flash light.

Firefly beetles flash light to attract a mate.

Female mosquitoes bite people, male mosquitoes don't.

LARVA

Beetles are insects with covers protecting their wings.

EGGS

When a ladybug hatches from an egg, it is a wingless larva.
It becomes a pupa then changes into an adult beetle with wings. In spring, the female lays eggs on plants.

These bees and wasps have two pairs of wings and stingers to protect themselves.

LADYBUG BEETLE

PUPA

Sounds you hear in the backyard may be grasshoppers, crickets or cicadas, trying to attract mates.

Ants live together in nests. The queen lays eggs that hatch into worker ants. They find food, guard the nest, and care for the young.

A praying mantis eats other insects.

By looking like a twig, a walkingstick fools insect eaters.

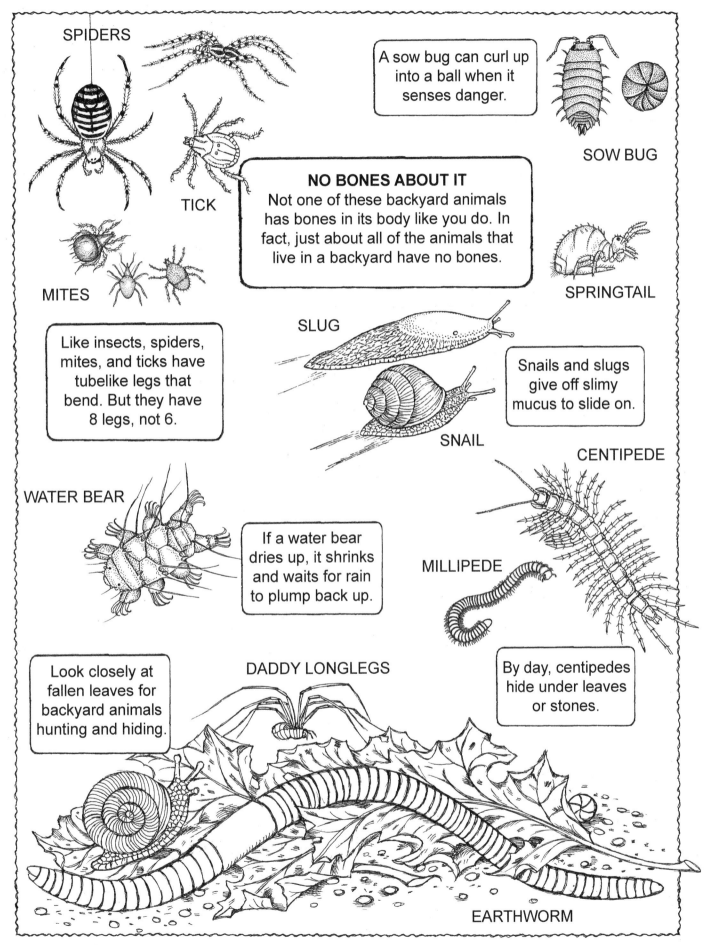

SPIDERS

A sow bug can curl up into a ball when it senses danger.

SOW BUG

TICK

**NO BONES ABOUT IT**
Not one of these backyard animals has bones in its body like you do. In fact, just about all of the animals that live in a backyard have no bones.

SPRINGTAIL

MITES

SLUG

Like insects, spiders, mites, and ticks have tubelike legs that bend. But they have 8 legs, not 6.

Snails and slugs give off slimy mucus to slide on.

SNAIL

CENTIPEDE

WATER BEAR

If a water bear dries up, it shrinks and waits for rain to plump back up.

MILLIPEDE

Look closely at fallen leaves for backyard animals hunting and hiding.

DADDY LONGLEGS

By day, centipedes hide under leaves or stones.

EARTHWORM

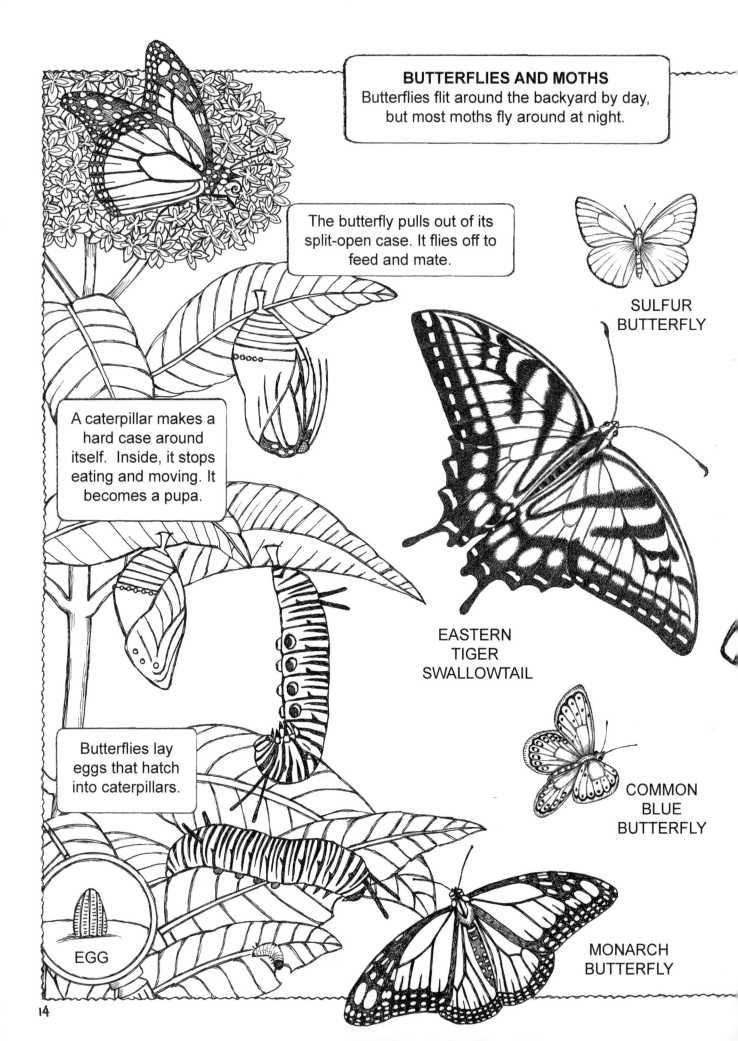

**BUTTERFLIES AND MOTHS**
Butterflies flit around the backyard by day, but most moths fly around at night.

The butterfly pulls out of its split-open case. It flies off to feed and mate.

SULFUR
BUTTERFLY

A caterpillar makes a hard case around itself. Inside, it stops eating and moving. It becomes a pupa.

EASTERN
TIGER
SWALLOWTAIL

Butterflies lay eggs that hatch into caterpillars.

COMMON
BLUE
BUTTERFLY

EGG

MONARCH
BUTTERFLY

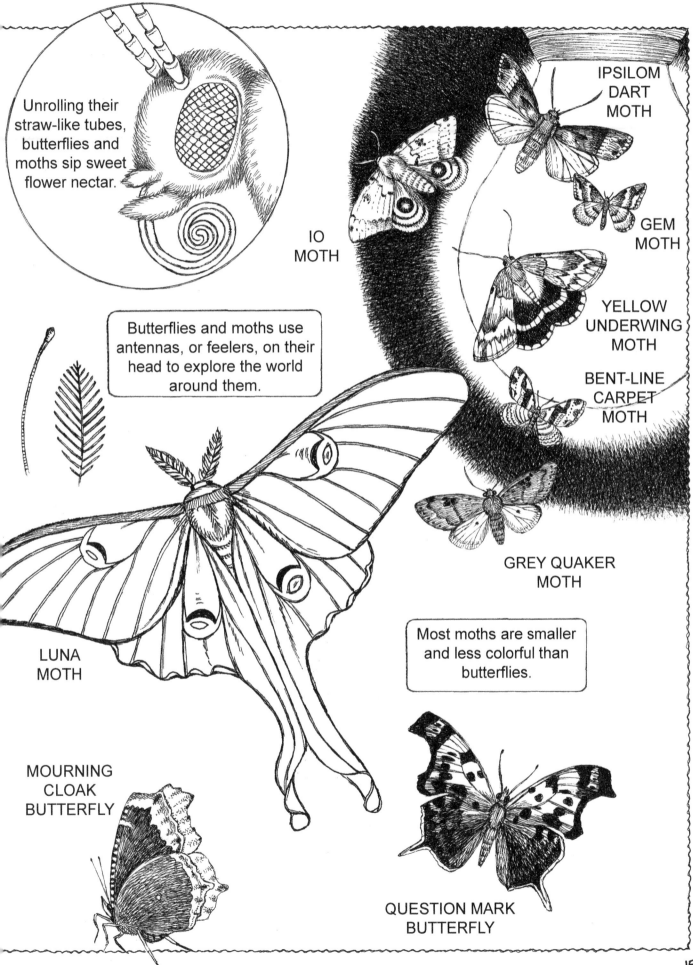

Unrolling their straw-like tubes, butterflies and moths sip sweet flower nectar.

IO MOTH

IPSILOM DART MOTH

GEM MOTH

YELLOW UNDERWING MOTH

BENT-LINE CARPET MOTH

Butterflies and moths use antennas, or feelers, on their head to explore the world around them.

GREY QUAKER MOTH

LUNA MOTH

Most moths are smaller and less colorful than butterflies.

MOURNING CLOAK BUTTERFLY

QUESTION MARK BUTTERFLY

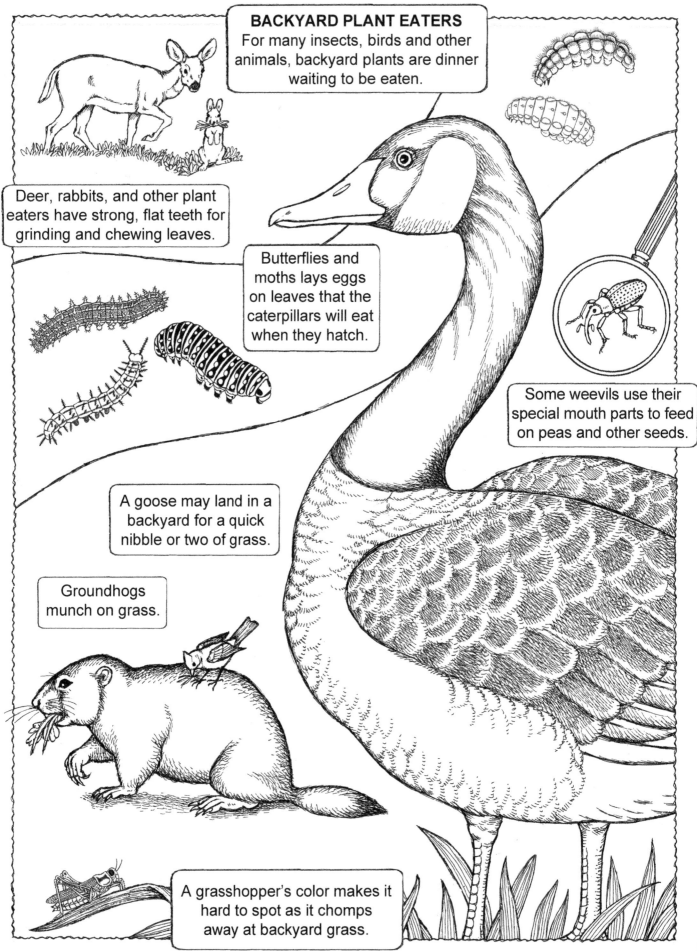

**BACKYARD PLANT EATERS**
For many insects, birds and other animals, backyard plants are dinner waiting to be eaten.

Deer, rabbits, and other plant eaters have strong, flat teeth for grinding and chewing leaves.

Butterflies and moths lays eggs on leaves that the caterpillars will eat when they hatch.

Some weevils use their special mouth parts to feed on peas and other seeds.

A goose may land in a backyard for a quick nibble or two of grass.

Groundhogs munch on grass.

A grasshopper's color makes it hard to spot as it chomps away at backyard grass.

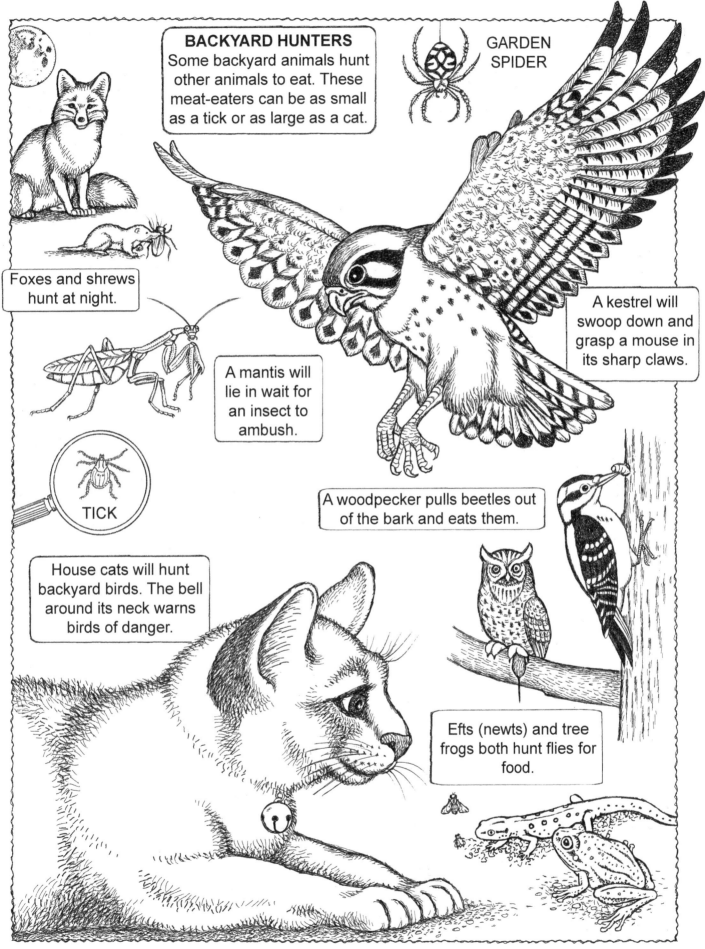

**BACKYARD HUNTERS**
Some backyard animals hunt other animals to eat. These meat-eaters can be as small as a tick or as large as a cat.

GARDEN SPIDER

Foxes and shrews hunt at night.

A mantis will lie in wait for an insect to ambush.

TICK

A kestrel will swoop down and grasp a mouse in its sharp claws.

A woodpecker pulls beetles out of the bark and eats them.

House cats will hunt backyard birds. The bell around its neck warns birds of danger.

Efts (newts) and tree frogs both hunt flies for food.

Tent caterpillars spin a large silk tent around them for protection. By day they leave it to find food; at night they return.

## NESTS
Some animals build nests in backyards to lay eggs and raise their young. Others build nests to live in all year long.

Wasps, such as hornets, chew wood and make a papery nest from it. Stay away from a hornet's nest – the wasps will sting.

House sparrows make nests of twigs on walls of buildings and even in street lights.

Hang a bat house and a bat may move in and eat backyard insects.

A mother raccoon finds a safe place in trees (or attics!) to give birth and raise her babies.

Most squirrels build big leaf nests in trees, but some, like the chipmunk, dig burrows in the ground.

Robins build nests hidden in trees, where its babies will be safe from predators.

In the nest they built, thousands of ants live together ruled by a queen. The queen's job is to lay eggs.

**SUMMER**
Summer is the warmest season of the year. Plant eaters have plenty of food to nibble on and predators have little trouble finding prey to eat.

Honeybees fly from flower to flower sipping sweet nectar and collecting pollen.

What's the robin waiting for? An earthworm to catch for dinner, of course!

If a grasshopper senses danger, it will spring to safety using its long, jumping legs.

A toad's sticky tongue will capture the tasty fly.

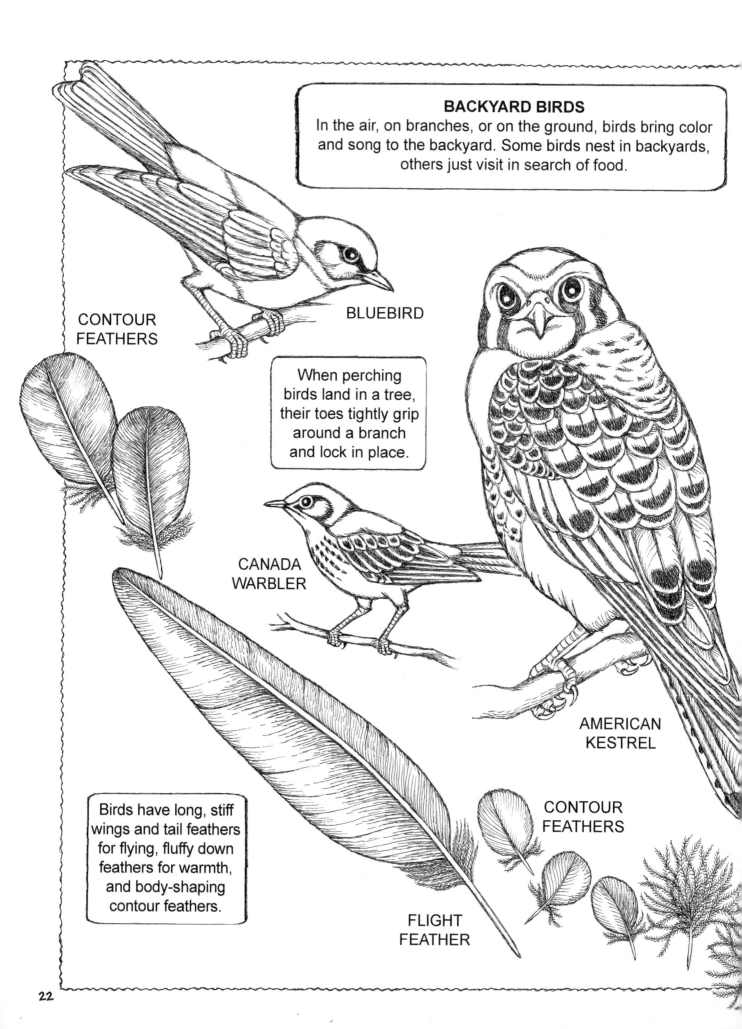

**BACKYARD BIRDS**
In the air, on branches, or on the ground, birds bring color and song to the backyard. Some birds nest in backyards, others just visit in search of food.

CONTOUR
FEATHERS

BLUEBIRD

When perching birds land in a tree, their toes tightly grip around a branch and lock in place.

CANADA
WARBLER

AMERICAN
KESTREL

CONTOUR
FEATHERS

Birds have long, stiff wings and tail feathers for flying, fluffy down feathers for warmth, and body-shaping contour feathers.

FLIGHT
FEATHER

Armed with hooked beaks, keen eyesight, and sharp, curved claws, hawks and owls hunt down mice and other small backyard animals to eat.

Hooked and sharp beak for meat eating

SCREECH OWL

Chisel-shaped beak for drilling for insects

Birds have different kinds of toothless beaks for getting the kinds of food they need to eat.

Pointed beak for catching insects

HOUSE WREN

Straw-shaped beak for sipping flower nectar

Cone–shaped beak for cracking seeds

Wide beak for trapping flying insects

HERMIT THRUSH

DOWN FEATHERS

A hermit thrush searches for worms.

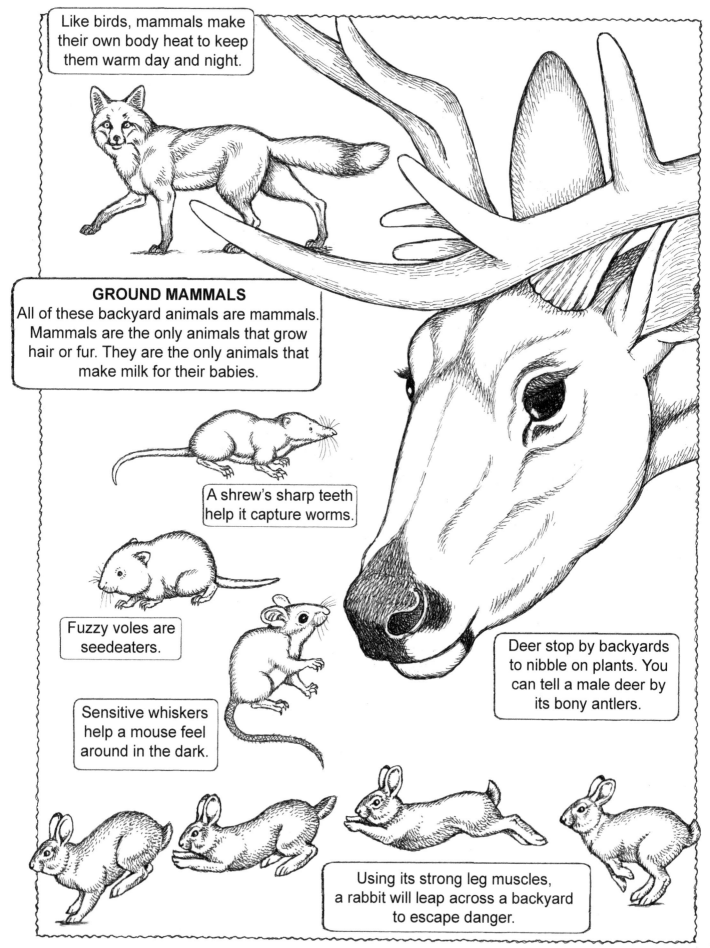

Like birds, mammals make their own body heat to keep them warm day and night.

**GROUND MAMMALS**
All of these backyard animals are mammals. Mammals are the only animals that grow hair or fur. They are the only animals that make milk for their babies.

A shrew's sharp teeth help it capture worms.

Fuzzy voles are seedeaters.

Sensitive whiskers help a mouse feel around in the dark.

Deer stop by backyards to nibble on plants. You can tell a male deer by its bony antlers.

Using its strong leg muscles, a rabbit will leap across a backyard to escape danger.

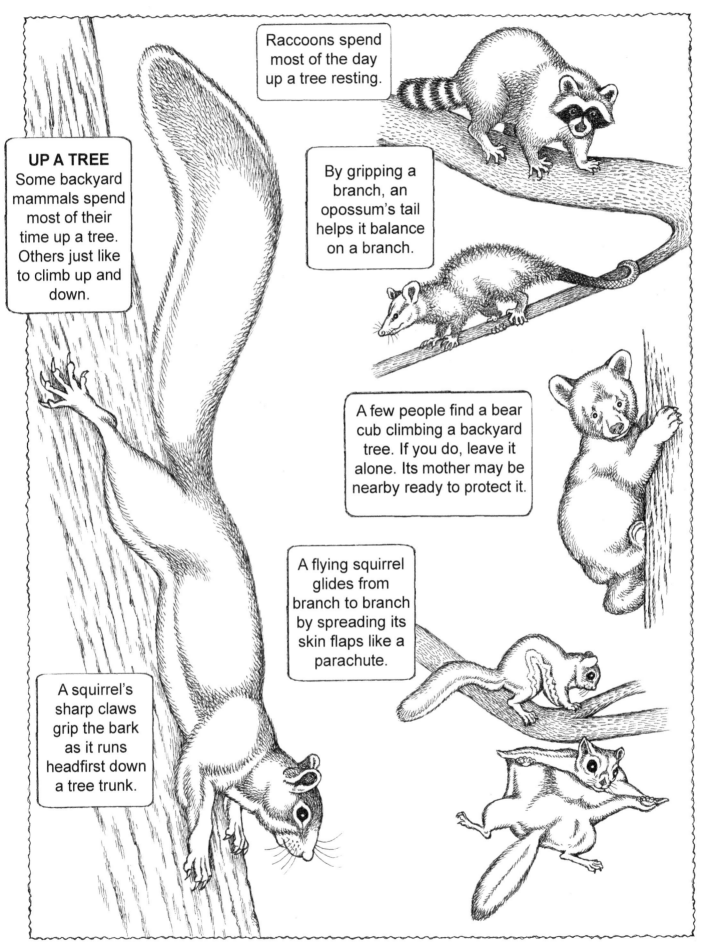

Raccoons spend most of the day up a tree resting.

**UP A TREE**
Some backyard mammals spend most of their time up a tree. Others just like to climb up and down.

By gripping a branch, an opossum's tail helps it balance on a branch.

A few people find a bear cub climbing a backyard tree. If you do, leave it alone. Its mother may be nearby ready to protect it.

A flying squirrel glides from branch to branch by spreading its skin flaps like a parachute.

A squirrel's sharp claws grip the bark as it runs headfirst down a tree trunk.

**FINDING FOOD**
All animals must find food to stay alive. Some animals eat backyard plants. Others eat the animals that eat the plants. And still others eat both plants and animals.

Foxes, falcons, and owls are predators – they hunt other animals to eat.

A woodpecker hammers away at tree bark in search of insects.

The raccoon feeds on plants and animals.

Many caterpillars munch on leaves but butterflies and moths sip sweet flower nectar.

Mice and chipmunks nibble on plants and seeds to get nutrients for energy.

Recyclers get their nutrients by breaking down dead plants and animals.

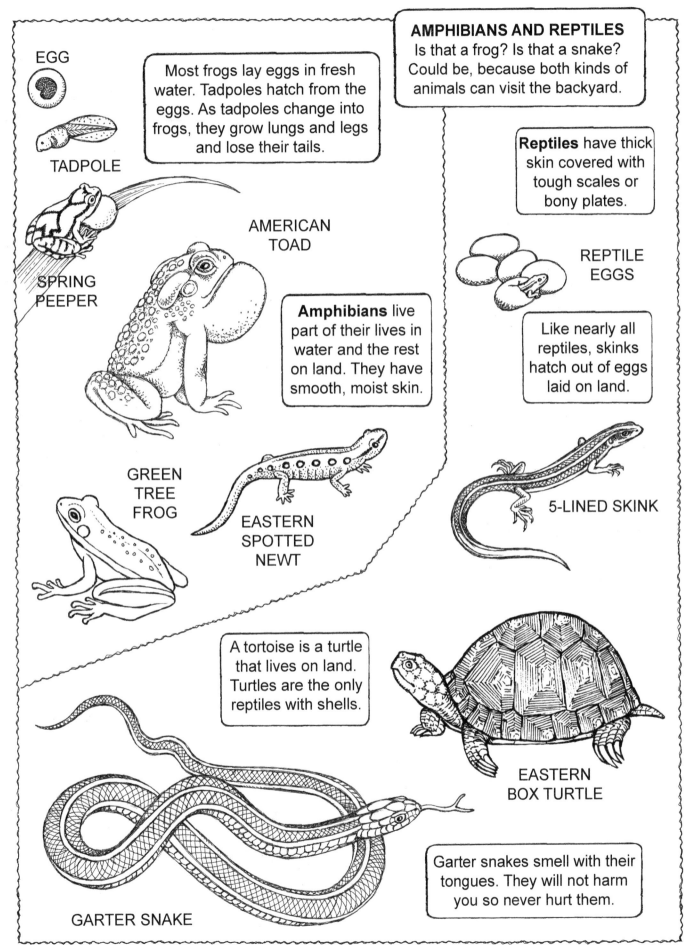

EGG

TADPOLE

Most frogs lay eggs in fresh water. Tadpoles hatch from the eggs. As tadpoles change into frogs, they grow lungs and legs and lose their tails.

SPRING PEEPER

**AMPHIBIANS AND REPTILES**
Is that a frog? Is that a snake? Could be, because both kinds of animals can visit the backyard.

**Reptiles** have thick skin covered with tough scales or bony plates.

AMERICAN TOAD

REPTILE EGGS

**Amphibians** live part of their lives in water and the rest on land. They have smooth, moist skin.

Like nearly all reptiles, skinks hatch out of eggs laid on land.

GREEN TREE FROG

EASTERN SPOTTED NEWT

5-LINED SKINK

A tortoise is a turtle that lives on land. Turtles are the only reptiles with shells.

EASTERN BOX TURTLE

Garter snakes smell with their tongues. They will not harm you so never hurt them.

GARTER SNAKE

A Canada warbler flies in to feed on its way to its warm winter home.

Look for the hard cases caterpillars make around them in autumn.

Red-orange monarch butterflies turn this hickory tree into a rest stop as they fly south for winter.

The squirrel is busy collecting and hiding acorns for winter.

The luna moth spends autumn and winter as a caterpillar.

A newt may hide in a pile of backyard leaves.

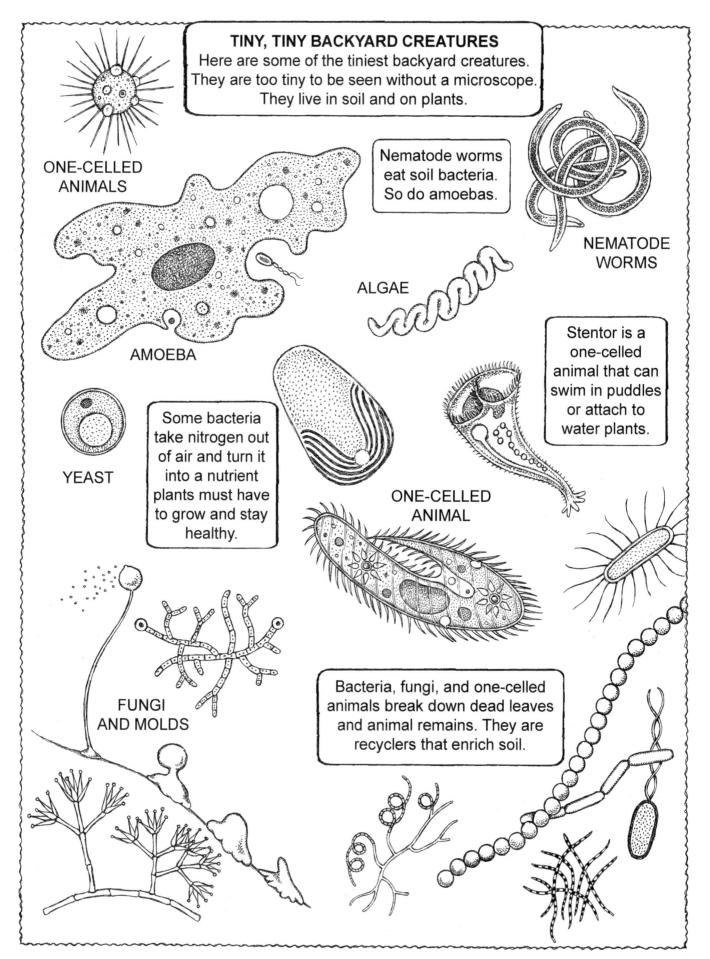

**TINY, TINY BACKYARD CREATURES**
Here are some of the tiniest backyard creatures.
They are too tiny to be seen without a microscope.
They live in soil and on plants.

ONE-CELLED
ANIMALS

Nematode worms
eat soil bacteria.
So do amoebas.

NEMATODE
WORMS

ALGAE

AMOEBA

Stentor is a
one-celled
animal that can
swim in puddles
or attach to
water plants.

YEAST

Some bacteria
take nitrogen out
of air and turn it
into a nutrient
plants must have
to grow and stay
healthy.

ONE-CELLED
ANIMAL

FUNGI
AND MOLDS

Bacteria, fungi, and one-celled
animals break down dead leaves
and animal remains. They are
recyclers that enrich soil.

**THE BACKYARD AT NIGHT**
At night the backyard may seem quiet, but don't be fooled. Animals that hid and rested during the day are on the move in search of food.

When very high sounds from a bat hit a moth, they echo back to the bat. The bat zooms in and captures the moth for dinner.

An owl can hear a mouse squeak and pinpoint where it is.

Raccoons eat just about anything: plants, frogs, insects, mice, even food in trash cans.

Fireflies blink light to attract each other.

A mouse's whiskers help it feel its way through the yard in the dark.

An earthworm pulls a leaf into its tunnel.

## MUSHROOMS

Mushrooms aren't plants. They don't make food, they don't grow flowers, and they don't make seeds. They are fungi. So are molds and yeasts.

Never eat mushrooms you find growing. Some, like amanita mushrooms, are poisonous.

A puffball mushroom puffs out thousands of tiny brown specks that can grow into a new mushroom.

A bracket fungus gets its food by breaking down the wood it lives on.

Look for fawn mushrooms on rotting logs or tree stumps.

Like roots, the threads of morel mushrooms spread underground.

Those mushrooms growing in a ring are called fairy rings. They absorb food from the remains of dead plants and animals in the soil.

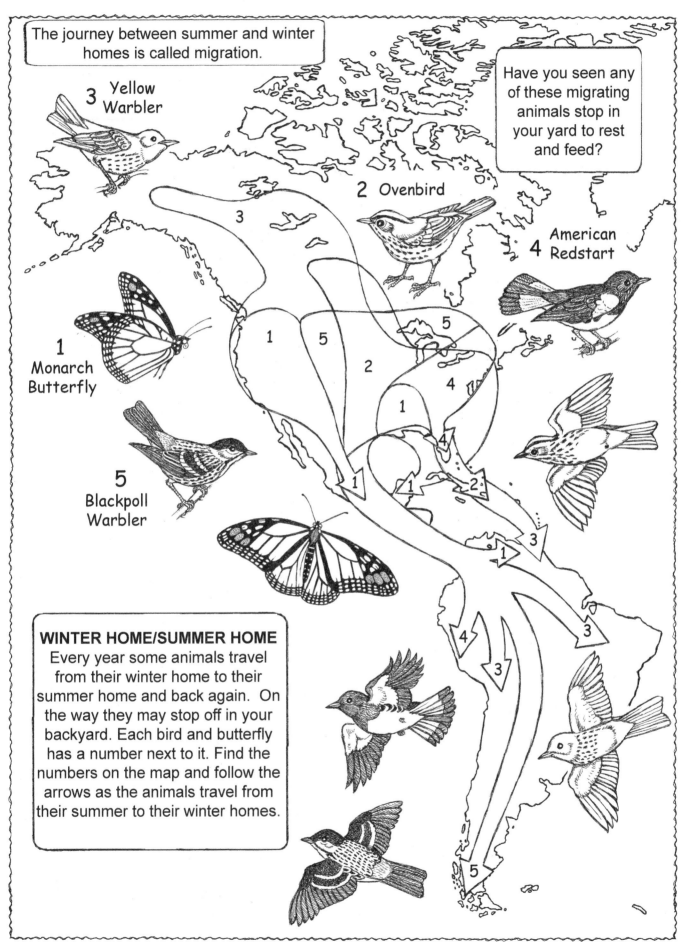

The journey between summer and winter homes is called migration.

Have you seen any of these migrating animals stop in your yard to rest and feed?

3 Yellow Warbler

2 Ovenbird

4 American Redstart

1 Monarch Butterfly

5 Blackpoll Warbler

**WINTER HOME/SUMMER HOME**
Every year some animals travel from their winter home to their summer home and back again. On the way they may stop off in your backyard. Each bird and butterfly has a number next to it. Find the numbers on the map and follow the arrows as the animals travel from their summer to their winter homes.

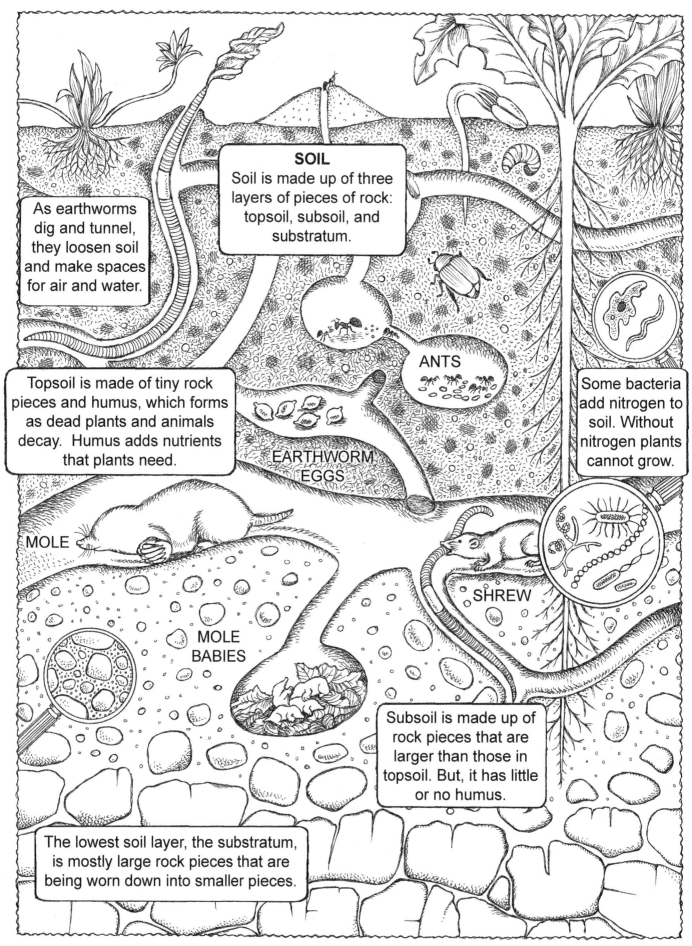

**SOIL**
Soil is made up of three layers of pieces of rock: topsoil, subsoil, and substratum.

As earthworms dig and tunnel, they loosen soil and make spaces for air and water.

Topsoil is made of tiny rock pieces and humus, which forms as dead plants and animals decay. Humus adds nutrients that plants need.

ANTS

EARTHWORM EGGS

Some bacteria add nitrogen to soil. Without nitrogen plants cannot grow.

MOLE

MOLE BABIES

SHREW

Subsoil is made up of rock pieces that are larger than those in topsoil. But, it has little or no humus.

The lowest soil layer, the substratum, is mostly large rock pieces that are being worn down into smaller pieces.

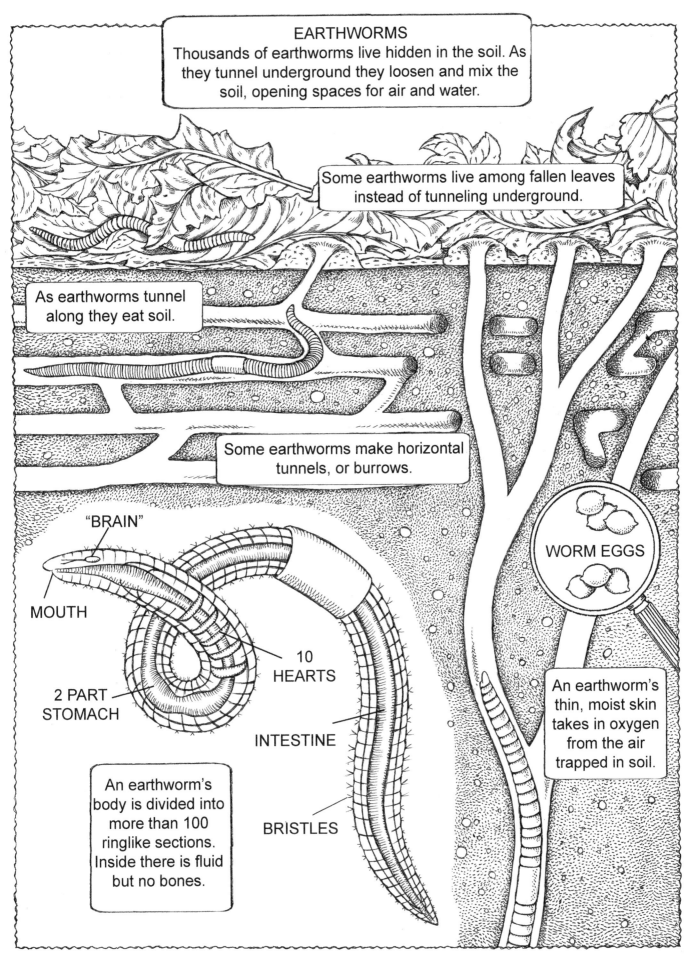

EARTHWORMS
Thousands of earthworms live hidden in the soil. As they tunnel underground they loosen and mix the soil, opening spaces for air and water.

Some earthworms live among fallen leaves instead of tunneling underground.

As earthworms tunnel along they eat soil.

Some earthworms make horizontal tunnels, or burrows.

WORM EGGS

"BRAIN"

MOUTH

2 PART STOMACH

10 HEARTS

INTESTINE

BRISTLES

An earthworm's body is divided into more than 100 ringlike sections. Inside there is fluid but no bones.

An earthworm's thin, moist skin takes in oxygen from the air trapped in soil.

35

LIFE IN THE FALLEN LEAVES
Hidden in the layer of fallen leaves are ants, snails, and other small animals. There they find food and shelter from the hot sun.

Millions of one-celled animals, fungi, and bacteria break down dead plants and animals into simple forms plants use to grow.

Insects lay eggs on animal droppings. When the eggs hatch, the young feed on the droppings.

Insects, snails, and millipedes munch on decaying leaves. Predators feed on the plant-eaters.

From dead plants and animals, recyclers make nutrient-rich humus.

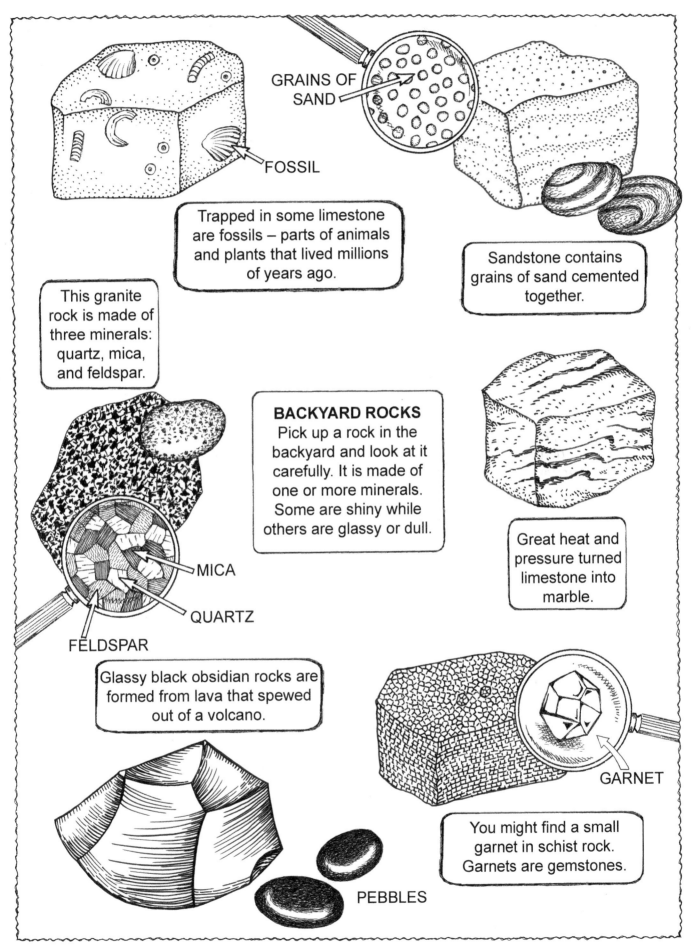

GRAINS OF SAND

FOSSIL

Trapped in some limestone are fossils – parts of animals and plants that lived millions of years ago.

Sandstone contains grains of sand cemented together.

This granite rock is made of three minerals: quartz, mica, and feldspar.

**BACKYARD ROCKS**
Pick up a rock in the backyard and look at it carefully. It is made of one or more minerals. Some are shiny while others are glassy or dull.

MICA

QUARTZ

FELDSPAR

Great heat and pressure turned limestone into marble.

Glassy black obsidian rocks are formed from lava that spewed out of a volcano.

GARNET

You might find a small garnet in schist rock. Garnets are gemstones.

PEBBLES

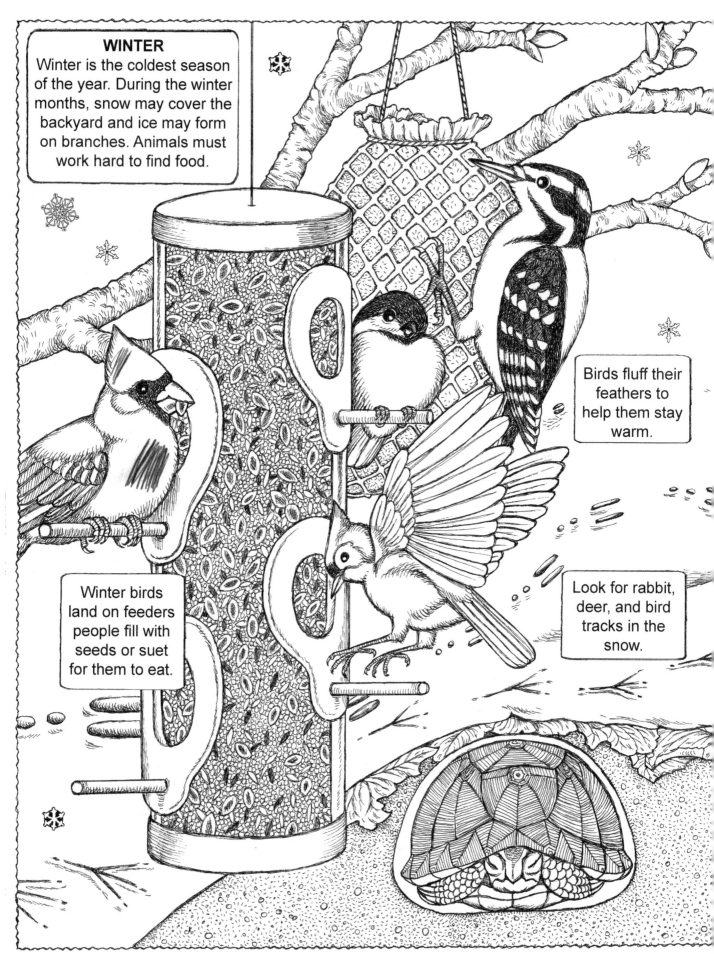

**WINTER**
Winter is the coldest season of the year. During the winter months, snow may cover the backyard and ice may form on branches. Animals must work hard to find food.

Birds fluff their feathers to help them stay warm.

Winter birds land on feeders people fill with seeds or suet for them to eat.

Look for rabbit, deer, and bird tracks in the snow.

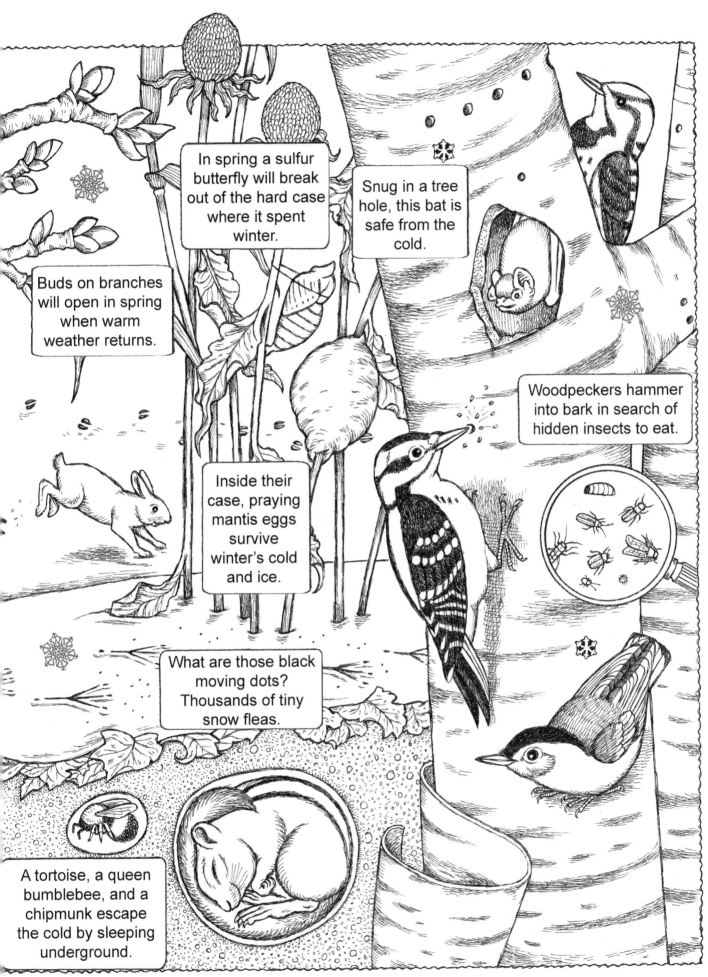

In spring a sulfur butterfly will break out of the hard case where it spent winter.

Snug in a tree hole, this bat is safe from the cold.

Buds on branches will open in spring when warm weather returns.

Woodpeckers hammer into bark in search of hidden insects to eat.

Inside their case, praying mantis eggs survive winter's cold and ice.

What are those black moving dots? Thousands of tiny snow fleas.

A tortoise, a queen bumblebee, and a chipmunk escape the cold by sleeping underground.

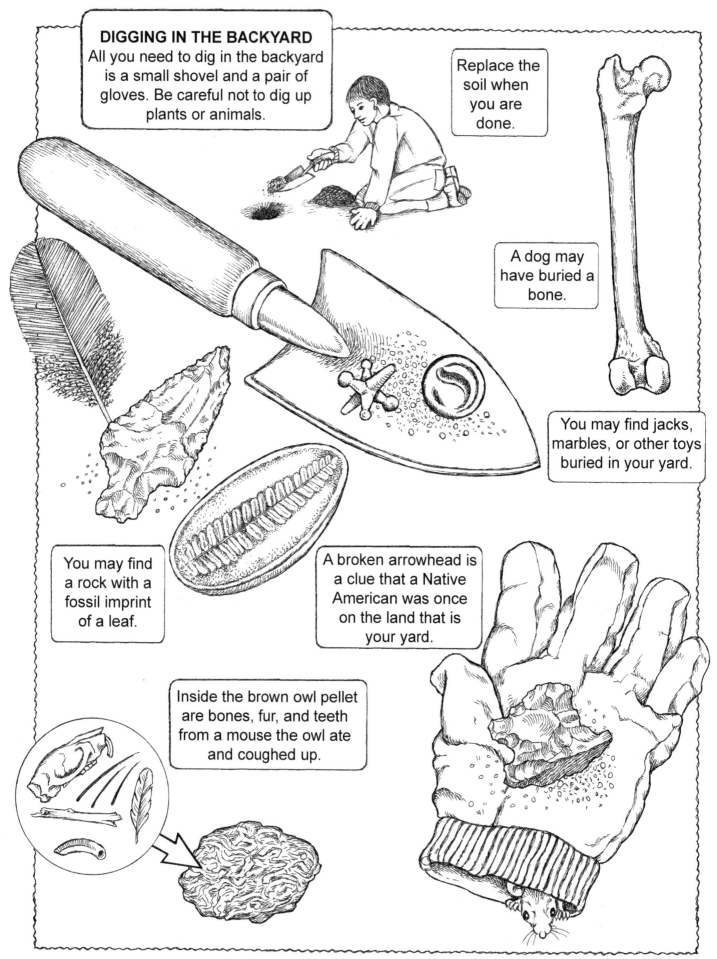

**DIGGING IN THE BACKYARD**
All you need to dig in the backyard is a small shovel and a pair of gloves. Be careful not to dig up plants or animals.

Replace the soil when you are done.

A dog may have buried a bone.

You may find jacks, marbles, or other toys buried in your yard.

You may find a rock with a fossil imprint of a leaf.

A broken arrowhead is a clue that a Native American was once on the land that is your yard.

Inside the brown owl pellet are bones, fur, and teeth from a mouse the owl ate and coughed up.

**PLANTING A TREE**
If you find an acorn in your backyard, you are on your way to growing a new oak tree.

In a single year thousands of acorns can drop from one oak tree.

Acorns are food for blue jays, deer, mice, and squirrels.

Acorns planted by you or hidden in the earth by squirrels can grow into trees.

Leaves sprout as the young oak grows.

The seedling pushes up out of the soil.

Inside an acorn is a seed that can grow into a new oak tree.

The seed sends down a root to absorb water and nutrients from the soil.

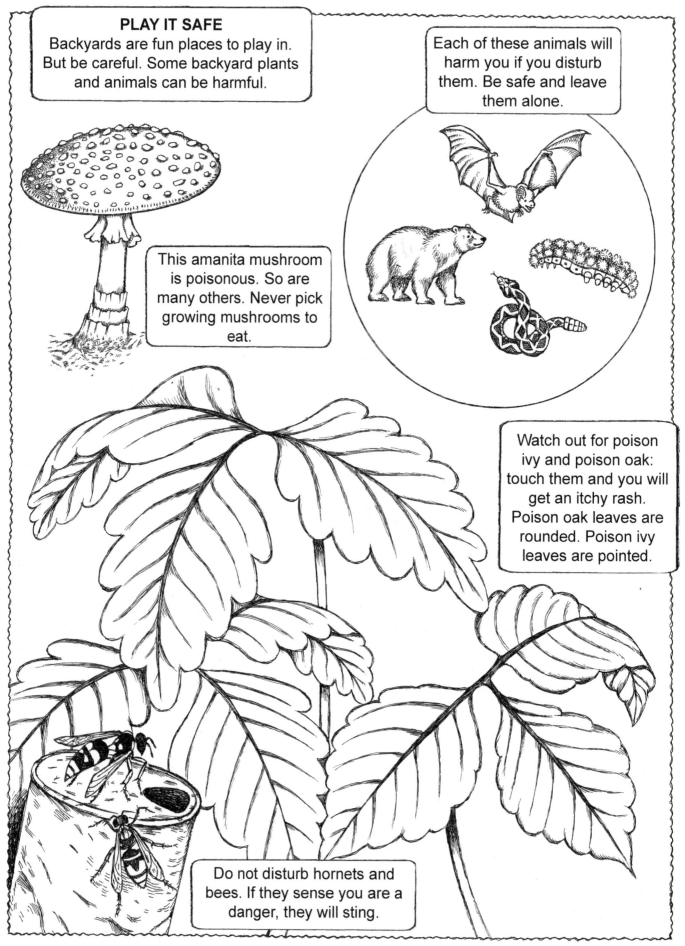

**PLAY IT SAFE**
Backyards are fun places to play in. But be careful. Some backyard plants and animals can be harmful.

Each of these animals will harm you if you disturb them. Be safe and leave them alone.

This amanita mushroom is poisonous. So are many others. Never pick growing mushrooms to eat.

Watch out for poison ivy and poison oak: touch them and you will get an itchy rash. Poison oak leaves are rounded. Poison ivy leaves are pointed.

Do not disturb hornets and bees. If they sense you are a danger, they will sting.

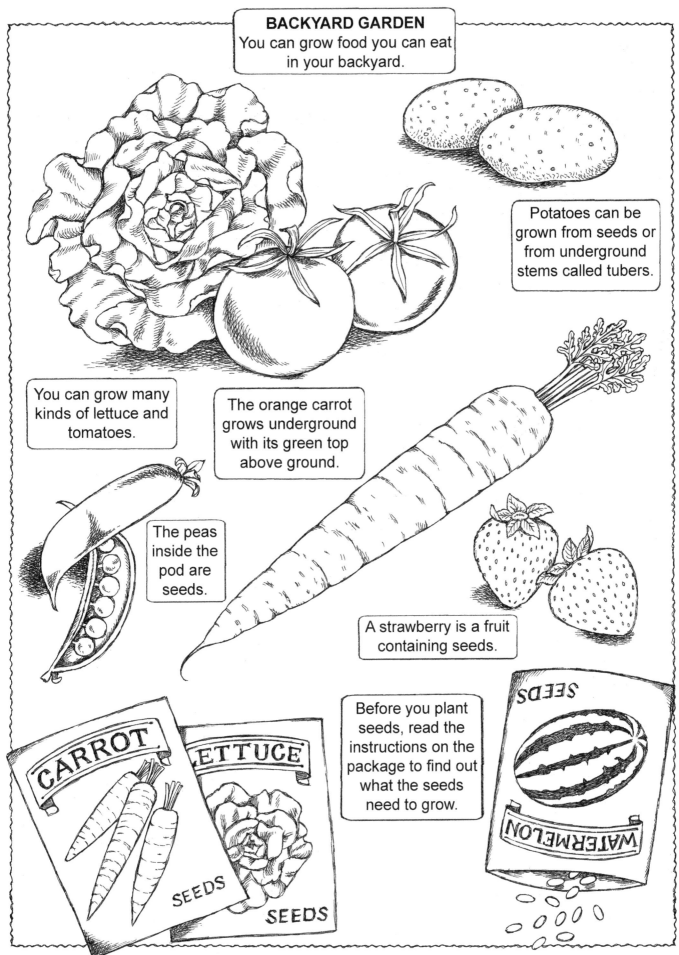

**BACKYARD GARDEN**
You can grow food you can eat in your backyard.

Potatoes can be grown from seeds or from underground stems called tubers.

You can grow many kinds of lettuce and tomatoes.

The orange carrot grows underground with its green top above ground.

The peas inside the pod are seeds.

A strawberry is a fruit containing seeds.

Before you plant seeds, read the instructions on the package to find out what the seeds need to grow.

CARROT

LETTUCE

SEEDS

SEEDS

SEEDS

WATERMELON

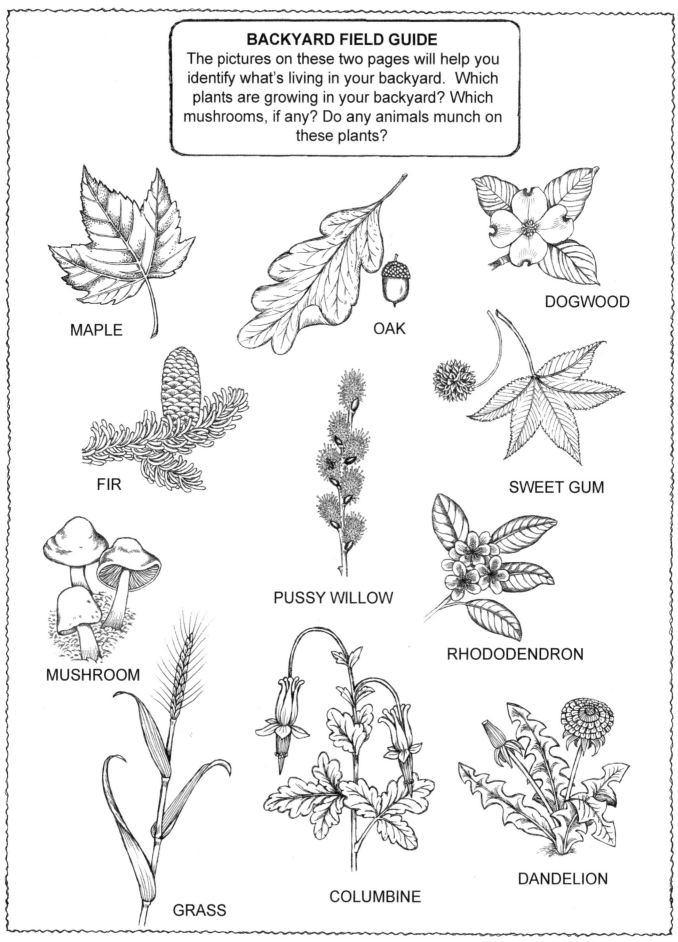

## BACKYARD FIELD GUIDE
The pictures on these two pages will help you identify what's living in your backyard. Which plants are growing in your backyard? Which mushrooms, if any? Do any animals munch on these plants?

MAPLE

OAK

DOGWOOD

FIR

PUSSY WILLOW

SWEET GUM

MUSHROOM

RHODODENDRON

GRASS

COLUMBINE

DANDELION

SPIDER

**BACKYARD FIELD GUIDE**
Which of these animals have you seen in your yard? What were they doing?

DOG

RACCOON

WARBLER

CAT

SNAIL

RABBIT

GRASSHOPPER

TORTOISE

FROG

BUTTERFLY

SKUNK

CHIPMUNK

OWL

45

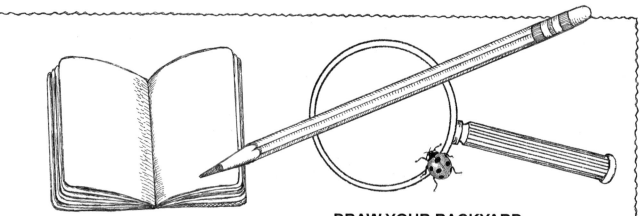

## DRAW YOUR BACKYARD
Draw a picture of what your backyard looks like. If you don't have a backyard, draw the kind of backyard you would like to have one day. Fill it with plants and animals.